WORLD HABITATS

GRASSLANDS

Rose Pipes

A ZOË BOOK

A ZOË BOOK

© 1997 Zoë Books Limited

Devised and produced by
Zoë Books Limited
15 Worthy Lane
Winchester
Hampshire SO23 7AB
England

First published in Great Britain in 1997 by
Zoë Books Limited
15 Worthy Lane
Winchester
Hampshire SO23 7AB

A record of the CIP data is available from the British Library.

ISBN 1 86173 016 0

Printed in Italy by Grafedit SpA
Editor: Kath Davies
Map: Sterling Associates
Design & Production: Sterling Associates

Photographic acknowledgments

The publishers wish to acknowledge, with thanks, the following photographic sources:

Environmental Images / Clive Jones 27; Robert Harding Picture Library / Explorer 21; The Hutchison Library 9 / Michael Kahn 6; / Robert Francis 10; / Vanessa Boeye 14; / Stephen Pern 15; Impact Photos / Neil Morrison 5; / John Cole 13; / Alain Le Garsmeur 16; / Javed A Jafferji 26; South American Pictures / Tony Morrison 18, 19, 20; Still Pictures / M & C Denis-Huot - cover background, 28; / Klein/Hubert - cover inset bl, 23; / Brigitte Marcon - cover inset tl; / Stephen Pern - title page, 17; / Hjalte Tin 7; / Mark Edwards 8; / Mikkel Ostergaard 25; TRIP / L Reemer 29; Zefa 11, 12, 22, 24.

The publishers have made every effort to trace the copyright holders, but if they have inadvertently overlooked any, they will be pleased to make the necessary arrangement at the first opportunity.

The publishers have made every effort to trace the copyright holders, but if they have inadvertently overlooked any, they will be pleased to make the necessary arrangement at the first opportunity.

Contents

What and where are grasslands?

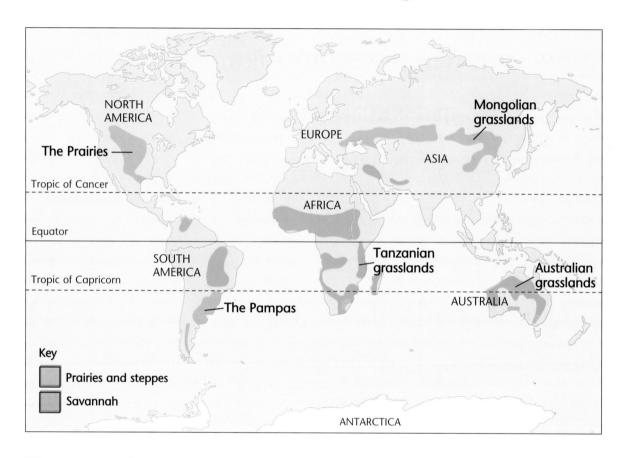

The map shows two sorts of grassland. Grasslands called savannah are in warm, dry lands. Grasslands called prairies, or steppes, are in cooler lands.

There may be no rain on the savannah for many months. Rain falls for part or most of the year in the prairies.

Wild grasses grow in parts of the world where it is too dry for forests to grow, and too wet for deserts to form.

This hippopotamus lives in Kenya, Africa. It eats the grass which is growing near the water. Wild grasses often grow in places that are flooded for part of the year.

Life in the grasslands

Grasslands are often flat places with few or no trees. The animals who live there have **adapted** to life in the grasslands.

Some birds use grass to make their nests. You can see a weaver bird's nest in this picture.

The soils and the weather on prairies and steppes are good for growing **crops** such as wheat, maize and barley. These crops are **cereals**. Their seeds, or grains, provide flour for making bread.

There are sheep and cattle farms on many grasslands. Meat, wool, milk, cheese and yoghurt are all important grassland **products**.

The farmland in this picture is in Estonia. Hundreds of years ago, this was wild grassland. Now it is an important area for growing crops.

In the savannah, the weather and the soils are not as good for growing crops as they are on the prairies and steppes.

This dry savannah grassland is in Burkina Faso in West Africa. Here, most people keep animals for meat, milk and skins. They also grow a few crops.

If rain does not fall for a long time, the grass and the crops may die from heat and lack of water. Grassland fires are also a danger in very dry summers.

Some wild grassland animals are in danger because people hunt and kill them. The hunters make money by selling the animals' skins, horns or tusks.

This is the Masai Mara **National Park** in Kenya, Africa. The animals are **protected** in this park.

The prairie of North America

Wild grassland once covered a large part of the United States of America and Canada. The North American grassland is called the prairie.

Today, there are farms on most of the prairie. This farmland is in the state of North Dakota in the USA. You can see the huge fields where cereals grow.

For hundred of years, the prairie was home to Native American peoples, and to millions of buffaloes and other wild animals.

About 150 years ago, people from Europe came to farm on the prairie. The new settlers wanted the land for themselves. They killed the buffaloes and drove away the Native Americans.

There are still some buffaloes on the prairie. They live in National Parks. This is Wind Cave National Park in South Dakota, USA.

When farming changed the grassland **habitat**, many wild animals lost their food and their homes. Wild grasses and other plants were ploughed up.

These prairie dogs live on the prairie. They make burrows in the ground and, like rabbits and coyotes, they eat grasses and cereals.

In the driest parts of the prairie, rain may not fall for many months. The soil dries out and turns into dust. These areas are called **dustbowls**. If there are strong winds, they will blow away the dust, and the soil is lost.

If the fields are on sloping ground, the farmers plough the soil around the slopes, not up and down. This helps to stop rain from washing away the soil.

Prairie farmers now plant trees around their fields. The trees shelter the land from very strong winds.

The grasslands of Mongolia

No trees grow on the flat, high grasslands, or steppes, of Mongolia. It is a hard place to live.

In summer it is very hot on these steppes. The winters are bitterly cold and windy, and snow may fall. The animals you can see are goats and yaks. Yaks are a type of cattle. They provide milk, skins and meat.

Some people who live on the Mongolian steppes keep herds of animals. These herders are **nomads**. They move around to find food for their animals.

The herders live in tents called yurts. A woollen cloth called felt covers the wooden poles to form a shelter.

These herders have just milked their goats. The woman is carrying the milk in a bucket to her yurt.

The herders use milk from their animals to make foods such as cheese and yoghurt. They buy other food in the towns, where they sell their animal skins, meat, wool and horses.

A Mongolian herder with his horses

Nearly half the people of Mongolia live and work on farms, or **ranches**, in the grasslands.

Large numbers of ranch animals are eating the grass and wearing away the soil on the steppes. In the driest parts the ranchlands are in danger of turning into desert.

When the grass has gone, there is nothing to hold down, or anchor, the soil. It turns into dust, which the strong winds blow away easily. The area becomes a desert.

The pampas of Argentina

The Spanish people who settled in Argentina called the grasslands the 'pampas'. The pampas soils are rich, and plenty of rain falls on them. It is good land for farming. Many of the huge farms are cattle or sheep ranches.

People began to farm on the pampas about 400 years ago. Before that time, the grassland grew wild. Wolves called 'maned wolves' once lived there.

Today, farmers grow cereals and other crops in the wetter parts of the pampas. Cattle and sheep graze on ranches in the drier areas.

When the farmers grew crops, the wolves' habitat changed. Maned wolves like this one moved to live in the woodlands of southern Brazil.

The rhea is the largest bird in South America. It is well adapted to living on wide open grasslands. It eats grass and other plants, as well as insects and small **mammals**. The rhea cannot fly, but it can run very fast.

Cowboys, called 'gauchos' in Spanish, used to live and work on the pampas. The gauchos rode horses to round up cattle and sheep on the ranches.

Very few gauchos work on the pampas today. At **festivals** men dress up and ride like the gauchos.

The grasslands of Australia

Nearly half of the land in Australia is desert. Most of the rest of the land is grassland. The picture shows grassland in Australia. The hills of earth are the nests of insects called termites.

In some of the wildest areas, the grassland habitat has not changed for thousands of years. Many wild animals still live in these areas.

The kangaroo is one of the largest wild animals living in the Australian grasslands. Kangaroos eat grass and other plants. They leap across the ground on their long back legs.

Young kangaroos grow inside a pocket, or pouch, on their mother's body. Animals with pouches are called **marsupials**. Most of the world's marsupials live in Australia.

When the European settlers came to Australia, they brought sheep and cattle with them to graze on the grasslands.

Most of the sheep in Australia are Merinos, like these sheep. Merinos are famous for their fine wool. This wool is now sent, or **exported**, to countries all over the world.

Until about 200 years ago, the only people in Australia were the Aboriginal peoples. They lived a nomadic life on the grasslands. They hunted animals and gathered berries and plants to eat.

The European settlers treated these people very badly. Many Aboriginals died or were moved off the land.

Today, most Aboriginal people live in or near towns and cities. Some people, like those in this picture, work on farms.

The grasslands of Tanzania

The Masai people are cattle herders who live on the East African savannah. Their lands are in Kenya and Tanzania.

Masai women milk the cows. The children help to herd the cattle.

The Masai live in villages. In the dry season, they move around the grasslands with their cattle. They travel a long way to find grass for their cattle to eat.

Thorn trees and wild grasses grow on the savannah in Tanzania. There are very few farms here, so the wild grassland habitat has not changed much.

Millions of wild animals live on the savannah. Many of these animals are grass eaters, like these zebra and wildebeest.

About a quarter of Tanzania's land is in National Parks and **reserves**.

Thousands of tourists visit Tanzania's National Parks to see the wildlife.

Many of the larger mammals, such as this cheetah, eat meat. They run very fast to catch their food, or **prey**.

Tourists pay to travel in the National Parks. The money is used to look after the parks. It also helps to pay for people to study the wildlife there.

People can drive close to the animals, but it is not safe to walk around.

These tourists are in the Serengeti National Park. More than three million mammals live here. The world's largest bird lives here too. It is the ostrich, which cannot fly but it can run fast and kick hard.

Glossary

adapted: If a plant or an animal can find everything it needs to live in a place, we say that it has adapted to that place. The animals can find food and shelter, and the plants have enough food in the soil and enough water. Some animals have changed their shape or their colour over a long time, so that they can catch food or hide easily. Some plants in dry areas can store water in their stems or roots.

cereals: plants such as wheat and rice which produce grain. The cereals we eat for breakfast are made from these grain crops.

crops: plants which farmers grow to use or to sell.

dustbowl: an area of land where the soil has dried into dust.

exported: sold and taken to another country.

festival: a time when people remember something special in the past, or a special time of the year.

habitat: the natural home of a plant or animal. Examples of habitats are deserts, forests and wetlands.

mammals: the group of animals whose young feed on their mother's milk.

marsupials: animals that carry their young in a pouch. The young feed on their mother's milk.

National Parks: laws are passed to protect these lands and their wildlife from harm. National Parks are usually places with beautiful scenery and rare wildlife.

nomads: people who do not live in one place. They move around all the time. Nomads in desert areas usually live in tents.

prey: an animal which another animal hunts for food.

products: crops that we grow or goods that we make.

protected: kept safe from changes that would damage the habitat.

ranches: large farms where farmers keep cattle, sheep or other animals.

reserves: areas of land set aside for wildlife to live in.

Index